Stories of Jesus

Illustrated

By Roger Adcock
Revised by Elsiebeth McDaniel
Illustrated by Gordon King

SCRIPTURE PRESS PUBLICATIONS, Inc.
Wheaton, Illinois; Fullerton, California; Ajax, Ontario, Canada

Contents

The Coming of the
Prince of Peace

The story of Christmas with the angels, shepherds, wise men, and the Baby is repeated each year. Some people have heard many stories about the main characters. But to find the true story of Christmas, one must turn to the Bible to read what really happened.

The Angel's Message

Her name was Mary. She lived with her mother and father in the little town of Nazareth. She was going to be married to the village carpenter, Joseph. Mary probably knew how to bake bread and how to weave cloth. Her mother had taught her other things that she would need to know to have a home of her own. How happy Mary was as she thought about the day when she and Joseph would be married.

One day God sent an angel to the village where Mary lived. In fact, God sent him to see Mary and give her a wonderful message.

The angel Gabriel said, "Greetings! The Lord is with you."

Mary was frightened. After all, how many people did she know who had seen an angel?

"Don't be afraid," the angel said. "God wants you to know that something wonderful is going to happen to you. Very soon now you will have a Baby

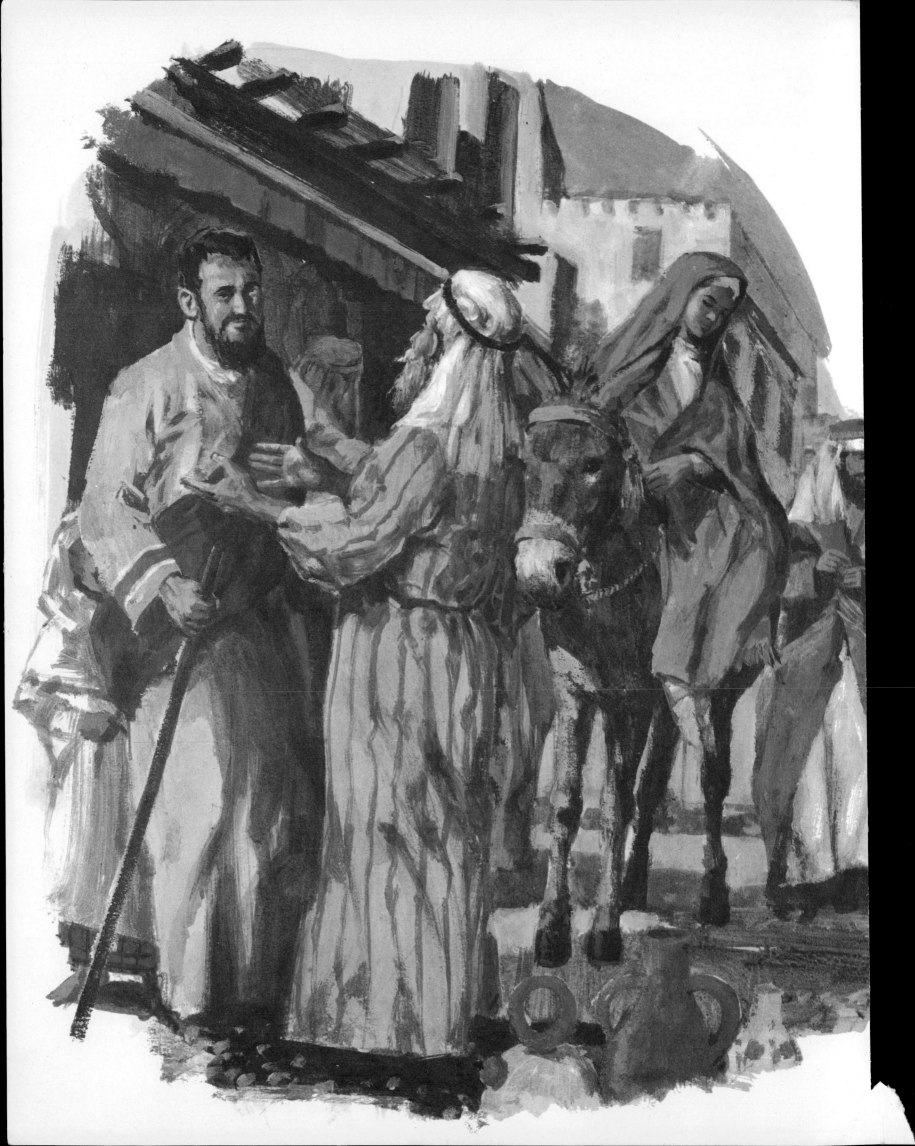

Boy, and you are to call Him Jesus. He will be very important and will be the very Son of God."

Mary did not understand all that the angel was saying, but she asked only one question. She said, "How can I have a baby? I am not married yet."

Then the angel told her, "The Holy Spirit of God will come to you, and the power of God shall be on you, and the Baby born to you will be the Son of God."

Mary said, "I am the Lord's servant. I am willing to do whatever He wants."

Then God's angel left Mary alone with her wonderful secret.

—*Luke 1:26-35*

Mary and Joseph Go to Bethlehem

Joseph loved Mary very much. They were going to be married. One night Joseph was thinking about his marriage to Mary when God caused him to fall asleep. As Joseph slept, he saw an angel standing beside him.

"Joseph, son of David," said the angel, "Mary will have a Son, and you shall name Him Jesus, for He will save His people from their sins."

When Joseph woke up, he remembered what God's angel had said, and he obeyed. Mary and Joseph were married. Then Mary went to Joseph's house to live with him and be his wife.

After Mary and Joseph were married, they lived in the little town of Nazareth. Joseph worked as a carpenter, and Mary took care of their house.

But one day some important news reached them. Joseph came to Mary and told her that the Emperor, Caesar Augustus, had made a new ruling. Messengers had brought his command to the town of Nazareth. And, of course, everyone had to obey the Emperor!

The rule or command said that everyone in the land had to register. And every man had to register in the city or town where his parents and grandparents had lived. For Mary and Joseph this command meant a long trip from Nazareth to Bethlehem. Bethlehem was the town where Joseph's family had lived.

The Emperor had made the rule so that he could have a list of all the families who lived in Palestine. Then when he had the list, he would make every family pay more taxes. He would know exactly who should pay.

Mary and Joseph started their long trip with other people who had to travel. Joseph must have locked up his carpenter's shop, and harnessed a donkey so that Mary could ride.

Mary and Joseph walked over mountains, along a river, and then over some hills. Joseph had made the trip before, and he could tell Mary interesting things about places as they came to them.

Finally Mary and Joseph reached Bethlehem. But they were not the only people who had come to Bethlehem to register. There were many, many more. So many people that by the time Mary and Joseph arrived, there were no more places to stay.

Joseph did find a place in a stable—a cave-like place where cattle were kept. It was not the best place for people to stay, but Mary was glad to get off the donkey, lie down in the straw, and rest.

And in that stable Mary's Son was born. She wrapped Him in long strips of cloth, as Bible-time mothers did, and laid Him in a manger. A manger looked like a large box without a top where feed for the cattle was placed. Mary and Joseph probably fixed straw in the manger to make it comfortable for the Baby Jesus. Of course, no cattle would eat from that manger! That manger was the very first bed the Lord Jesus had.

Meanwhile, in the fields around Bethlehem, some shepherds were watching their sheep. Shepherds had to guard their sheep so that no wild animals would come to kill or steal them.

Suddenly a great, dazzling light flashed across the fields. The shepherds were terribly afraid! As they tried to see what was happening, they saw an angel looking down at them from the sky. The angel said, "Don't be afraid! I bring you the best news that has ever been announced, and it is for everyone! In Bethlehem the Saviour has been born! How will you know Him? Well, you will find Him wrapped in long pieces of cloth, as newborn babies are wrapped, and lying in a manger."

Then many more angels joined the angel-messenger. The sky seemed to be filled with a whole army of shining angels. And all the angels began to praise God. "Glory to God in the highest heaven," they said, "and on Earth peace to men in whom God is well pleased."

Then the army of angels went back to heaven. The shepherds looked at one another, but it did not take them long to make up their minds. "Come on!" they said. "Let us go to Bethlehem right away. Let's see this wonderful thing that God has told us about."

God Himself must have helped the shepherds find the very place where Baby Jesus was lying in a manger. When they found the stable, the shepherds crowded in to see Jesus and worship Him.

Then the shepherds went back again to their sheep. On the way they told everyone what had happened and what the angels had said about the new Baby. But Mary, Jesus' mother, quietly thought about all that had happened as she looked at Baby Jesus, God's Son.

—*Matthew 1:20-24; Luke 2:1-20*

The Wise Men Visit Jesus

Although Jesus was born in a stable and slept in a manger, He had some very important visitors. These visitors came from faraway. Many people think that the wise men came from Iran.

How did the wise men hear about Jesus? Well, the wise men studied the stars. They did not have instruments as astronomers do today, but they knew a great deal about the stars and their movements.

The people of that time believed that when some special event was to take place, strange new stars suddenly appeared in the heavens, shone for a time, and then disappeared.

One night the wise men were looking at the stars when they suddenly saw a new star. Perhaps the star looked larger or shone more brightly. The wise men thought the new star was very important —so important that they decided to follow it to see what great thing had happened. The men packed their camels with clothing, food, and special gifts. Probably they did not know then that their trip would take them more than one thousand miles away to Bethlehem.

Finally the wise men reached Jerusalem, the capital city of Palestine. There they began asking questions. "Where is the newborn King?" they asked. "We have seen His star far away in our land. Now we have come to worship Him."

When King Herod, the king of the country, heard their questions, he was upset! He was the king! How could there be another king?

King Herod called a meeting of the religious leaders to ask whether they knew anything about a new king. Some of them said, "Well, the Holy Scriptures say that some day a ruler will be born in Bethlehem."

King Herod immediately sent for the wise men. He asked them about the star they had seen. "When did you see it?" he asked.

After the wise men told Herod all that they knew about the star, he said, "Go to Bethlehem. Look for the Child. And when you have found Him, come back and tell me. I want to worship Him too!"

The wise men started out once more, and the star appeared to show them the way. When they reached Bethlehem, the star seemed to stop over one place. The wise men went into the house and found the little Boy with His mother, Mary. These great wise men, who were probably kings, knelt down and worshiped Jesus. They opened their packs and gave Him special gifts—gold, frankincense, and myrrh.

Although the wise men had found Jesus and worshiped Him, they did not take the news back to King Herod. God warned them in a dream to take another way to their homes.

Soon after the wise men left, God sent an angel to Joseph, Mary's husband. "Get up at once," said the angel. "Take the Child and His mother to Egypt. Stay there till God tells you to come back. King Herod is going to start looking for Jesus, and if he finds the Child, he will most certainly kill Him."

So Joseph got up in the middle of the night and started off for Egypt, just as God's angel had told him to do. Mary and Joseph and Jesus reached Egypt without any trouble from King Herod. And they lived safely in Egypt because King Herod had no power there.

—*Matthew 2:1-14*

Baby Jesus Goes to the Temple

Mary and Joseph loved God. They wanted to obey Him. They knew that God had said in the Holy Scriptures, "If your first child is a boy, he shall be set aside or given to Me in a special way."

How would Mary give her Son to God? She did it in the very same way that other Jewish mothers did. On the day that Jesus was forty days old, He was taken to the Temple in Jerusalem. Of course, this trip to Jerusalem took place between the time that the shepherds came to worship Jesus and the night when Joseph took Mary and Jesus to Egypt.

When Mary and Joseph went to the Temple, they made a sacrifice to the Lord. Then they went to a special service which showed that they were giving Jesus to God and promising to bring Him up to please and obey God.

The very day that Mary and Joseph were at the Temple, a very good man, named Simeon, came to the Temple. God had made a special promise to Simeon. He had promised that Simeon would not die until he had seen God's anointed King. God also let Simeon know that Jesus was that King.

When Simeon saw Mary and Joseph with Jesus, he took the Baby in his arms. Then he praised God. "Lord," he said, "now I can die content. I have seen the One You promised. I have seen the Saviour You are giving to the world."

—*Luke 2:22-31*

The Boy Jesus Goes to the Temple

Nazareth was a little town about one hundred miles from Jerusalem. When Mary and Joseph left Egypt, they went to live in Nazareth. There Jesus grew up.

Jesus' home must have been a busy one. Joseph worked hard in his carpenter shop. Mary was busy cooking food, weaving cloth, and sewing clothing for her family. And Jesus went to the synagogue school where He learned to read and write. Jesus played, helped Mary and Joseph, and studied hard.

Once every year many people from Nazareth made the trip to Jerusalem for the Passover Feast. The year that Jesus was twelve, Mary and Joseph took Him along to Jerusalem. Perhaps this was the first time Jesus had seen the beautiful Temple of God since He had been brought there as a Baby.

The trip to Jerusalem seemed to be like a parade. There were many people on the road. At night they camped by the side of the road. And it was fun to eat picnic meals on the way. Dates, melons, bread, and cheese tasted better than they did at home.

The children probably played a game, each one trying to be the first to see the city gates and the Temple. The Temple stood high above the city.

The Temple was not just one building but many. Hundreds of people could gather at one time in this huge place. It is hard to tell in words how very large and beautiful the Temple was.

The Passover Feast lasted several days. Then after the feast the people from Nazareth started home again. There were many people traveling

along the road. Mary and Joseph did not miss Jesus the first day. They probably thought that He was with some of His friends or relatives. But when He couldn't be found that evening, they began to worry. Perhaps Mary said to Joseph, "Joseph, I think we'd better turn back to Jerusalem. Jesus must be somewhere along the road. We'll have to find Him."

Mary and Joseph went back to Jerusalem. They looked everywhere for Jesus. Finally, on the third day of their search, they went to the Temple. They could see some teachers sitting on the steps.

"There are some teachers," said Mary. "Perhaps they have seen Jesus." Mary and Joseph hurried to ask the Temple teachers about Jesus. When they got to the teachers, there was Jesus. He was talking to the teachers.

Mary and Joseph did not know what to think when they saw Jesus sitting with the teachers and talking calmly with them. "Look," said Mary, "there He is."

To Jesus, Mary said, "Son, why have You done this to us? We have looked for You everywhere. We have looked for three days! Didn't You know we would worry about You?"

Jesus looked up at His mother's face with surprise. "But why did you need to look for Me? Didn't you know that I would be here in the Temple, talking about God?"

No, Mary and Joseph had not known that Jesus would be in the Temple. Perhaps they often forgot that Jesus was a special Boy. He was the very Son of God!

But without complaining or asking to stay, Jesus got up. He said good-bye to the teachers and left with Mary and Joseph. He obeyed and went back to Nazareth with them.

As Jesus grew up, He became taller and stronger. He learned more and more. But most important—He loved God and obeyed Him.

—Luke 2:41-52

Jesus and John

Jesus had a cousin named John. John was a very special person. His parents were given some important directions about him even before he was born. This is what happened.

One day John's father, Zacharias, was in the Temple in Jerusalem. Zacharias was a Jewish priest, and on this day it was his turn to burn incense on the golden altar in the Temple. Zacharias sprinkled the sweet-smelling incense on the hot coals, then he prayed as the sweet-smelling smoke was rising into the air. As Zacharias stood with his head bowed before God, suddenly an angel appeared on the right side of the altar of incense! Zacharias was afraid.

But the angel said to him, "Don't be afraid, Zacharias. God has heard your prayer." For what had Zacharias prayed? Both he and his wife, Elisabeth, wanted to have children, and they had often prayed that God would give them children. Now the angel said, "God has sent me to tell you that you and your wife will have a son. You are to name him John. You shall have joy and gladness, and many people shall be happy at his birth. Your son must never drink wine or beer. Your son will be one of the Lord's great men. He will tell many people to turn to the Lord God. He will teach people to love the Lord. And the Lord will fill him with His Spirit."

"But," said Zacharias, "this cannot be. My wife and I are very old. We are too old to have

15

children. How can I believe what you say unless you show me a sign?"

The angel answered, "I am Gabriel, who stands in the presence of God before His throne. God sent me with this special message of glad news. You should believe God's messenger without a sign. But because you have asked, I shall give you this sign. You shall not be able to speak till what I have said comes true." Then the angel disappeared.

When Zacharias left the Temple, he could not speak. At home he could not talk to Elisabeth. Perhaps he wrote the message that the angel had given to him.

About six months later, in the town of Nazareth, the angel Gabriel came to Mary. He told her that she was going to have a Baby, God's Son. She was to name the Baby Jesus. Then the angel told Mary some more good news. Even though Mary was Elisabeth's cousin, she did not know that Elisabeth was going to have a Baby too, so the angel told her. And Mary believed his message from the Lord.

After the angel left, Mary quickly got ready and hurried off to the town in Judaea where Zacharias and Elisabeth lived. How happy Mary was as she walked the many miles. When Mary got there, Elisabeth said, "Mary, you are blessed among all women. I know that you are to be the mother of God's Son."

Then Mary said, "My soul praises God. My spirit is glad because God is my Saviour. He has noticed me even though I am not an important person. He has blessed me. How wonderful and powerful God is!"

Mary stayed with Elisabeth until time for Elisabeth's baby to be born. The baby was a boy, just as the angel had said it would be.

When the baby was eight days old, friends and relatives came to dedicate the baby to the Lord. They wanted to call him Zacharias, the same name as his father had. But Zacharias shook his head. Then he asked for something to write on. Zacharias wrote, "The baby's name is John." The people were surprised.

John's father, Zacharias, knew the baby was special. After God caused Zacharias to be able to speak again, Zacharias said, "You, my baby boy,

will have special work to do. You will get people ready for the Saviour. You will tell people how to have their sins forgiven and turn to the Saviour."

When John grew up, he did preach about God. "Change your ways, people. Think about God!" he cried. "Ask God to forgive you for the wrong you have done," he called. "Be sorry for your sins! Tell God now, for the Lord is coming soon."

John lived outdoors and ate wild honey and roasted locusts. He did not do his preaching in a church, but outdoors. People were surprised to see that John the Baptist, as he was called, dressed in clothes made from camels' skins. The people had added "the Baptist" to John's name because he baptized many of them in the Jordan River.

What was the special work that God had asked John to do? John was to prepare the way for Jesus. He did this by telling people to be sorry for their sins and to ask God to forgive them. John was not afraid to tell people they were sinners. He called out to anyone who would listen, "Turn away from your sins! God is going to punish all sinners who will not come to Him!"

John also said, "There is One coming who is far greater than I am. He is so much greater that I am not even worthy to be His slave." These are the words John spoke to tell the people that Jesus, God's own Son, was soon to come.

The people who believed John's message were sorry for their sin. They asked John, "What should we do now?"

John told them exactly what they should do. "The person who has two coats should give one to the man who doesn't have any. The person who has more food than he needs should share with those who do not have food."

Tax collectors asked John what they should do. "Do not ask for more tax money than you are supposed to," said John.

Soldiers wondered what they should do. "Do not hurt any man. Do not arrest anyone who has not done wrong," John told them. "Don't complain because you don't earn more money."

One day, while John was preaching, he saw the Saviour Himself. Jesus, the wonderful Person John had said was coming, stood near. While John was preaching, Jesus stepped out of the crowd and stood before him. Jesus asked John to baptize Him. The two men went down to the river where John baptized Jesus. The Bible tells

something wonderful that happened right then.

When the two men were coming out of the water, the heavens opened and the Spirit of God in the form of a dove came down. The dove rested on Jesus. Then a voice spoke from heaven. God's

voice said, "You are My Son whom I love very much. You are My Son in whom I am well pleased."

Did all of the people hear the voice? Probably not, but they did hear what John the Baptist said next. He turned to the people and said, "Look, this Man is the Saviour who takes away the sin of the world. He is the very One I have told you about. He is much more important than I am. I was sent to tell you about Him and to get you ready to receive Him. He is Jesus, the Son of God!"

—*Mark 1:1-11; Luke 1:8-26, 39-49; John 1:29,34*

Jesus and the Tempter

After Jesus was baptized and ready to start His work for God, there was someone who was not pleased. In fact, he tried to make Jesus change His mind about serving God.

After Jesus was baptized, the Spirit of God led Him into the wilderness. The wilderness was a very lonely part of the country where no people lived. Only wild animals made their homes there. Perhaps Jesus found a cave among the rocks to use as His home during the forty days and nights He stayed there.

While Jesus was in the wilderness, the Devil, Satan, came to bother Him. Satan, or the Tempter, wanted to make Jesus stop serving God. He wanted Jesus to obey him instead. Satan knew that Jesus had not eaten anything during the time He was in the wilderness.

Satan, the Tempter, came to Jesus and suggested that He get some food for Himself. Satan said, "Change some of these stones into loaves of bread. That way You will prove that You are the Son of God."

Perhaps Jesus thought to Himself, "Yes, I am the Son of God. I do have power to change the stones into bread. And I am very hungry. But the power I have has not been given to Me to take care of Myself. It is not God's will that I should change the stones into bread."

Then Jesus repeated some Bible words, "Man shall not live by bread alone, but by every word

that God has spoken." Jesus said, "No, I will not change the stones into bread."

But Satan was not discouraged. The Tempter took Jesus into Jerusalem and then up, up to the highest part of the Temple. "Now," said Satan, "if you really want people to know that You are God's Son, throw Yourself down to the ground. The Scriptures say, 'He shall send His angels to keep You from harm.' The angels will keep You from being killed."

But Jesus said, "It is also written in the Scriptures, 'You shall not put God to a foolish test!'"

Still Satan did not give up! He took Jesus to the top of a very high mountain. There Satan was able to show Jesus all the nations of the world. Satan also showed Jesus all the power that He would have as Ruler of the world.

Satan said, "Look, I'll give You power over all the world if You'll just bow down and worship me. You can have everything!"

But Jesus said, "Go away from Me, Satan! It is written, 'You shall worship the Lord your God, and Him only shall you serve!' I want no more to do with you!"

Satan had lost! He could not make Jesus use His power for Himself. And He would not do anything just to show His power. Last of all, Jesus would not do as the Tempter wished even to be King over all the world.

When Satan knew that Jesus would not do anything he wanted, he left. Then God sent His angels to Jesus to give Him food.

Jesus left the wilderness and came back to Galilee, that part of Palestine where He had lived. There He began to be famous.

Jesus taught regularly in the synagogues, and people began to really listen to what He said. One day He read the Scripture lesson in the synagogue at Nazareth, which was His hometown. Each book of the Scriptures was written on a scroll, and Jesus was given the Book of Isaiah to read. So He unrolled the scroll until He found the place where these words were written:

"The Spirit of the Lord is upon Me. He has appointed Me to preach Good News to the poor. He has sent Me to announce that captives shall be freed from their owners. He has sent Me to announce that God is ready to give blessings to all who come to Him."

Then Jesus closed the scroll and sat down.

There was something about the way Jesus had read the Scripture that had made the people listen and think about what He had read. They wondered what He would say.

Jesus began by saying, "Today, even as you listened, these words of the Scripture have come true!"

All the people were surprised at what He said. Some said, "How can the words be true today? Isn't Jesus the son of Joseph, the carpenter?"

Some people believed Jesus. But some were very angry because Jesus had said the Scripture was true about Him. They wanted to push Him off a high cliff. But God gave Jesus power to walk through the crowd safely and leave them.

—*Luke 4:1-22, 28-30*

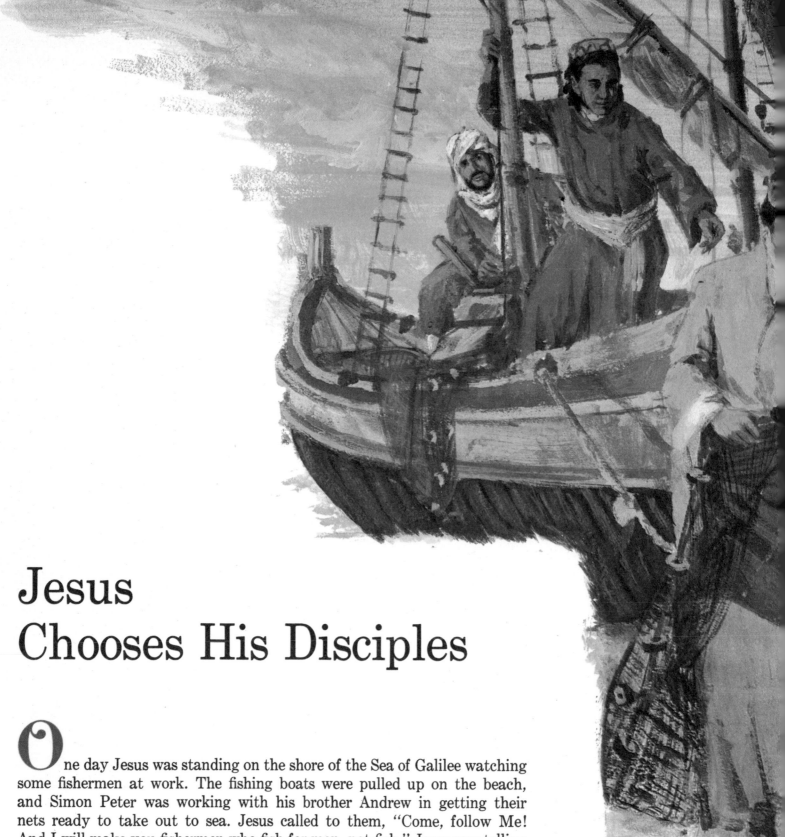

Jesus Chooses His Disciples

One day Jesus was standing on the shore of the Sea of Galilee watching some fishermen at work. The fishing boats were pulled up on the beach, and Simon Peter was working with his brother Andrew in getting their nets ready to take out to sea. Jesus called to them, "Come, follow Me! And I will make you fishermen who fish for men, not fish." Jesus was telling the men that they would help in His work of telling people about God.

A little farther up the beach, Jesus saw two other brothers—John and James. They were busy mending some holes in their net. Jesus called to them, "Come, follow Me!" And right away James and John left their nets, their boat, and their father who was in the boat with other fishermen. James and John were glad to become followers of the Lord Jesus.

One day sometime later Simon Peter had a chance to let the Lord Jesus use his fishing boat. Jesus was preaching on the shore of the lake. Great crowds of people stood around Jesus. In fact, the crowd was so big that many people could not see Jesus.

Simon Peter's boat was pulled up on the beach, and he was sitting in it. Jesus stepped into the boat and said to Peter, "Please push your boat out from the shore." Jesus knew that He could sit down in the boat, and the people would be able to see Him and hear what He said.

When Jesus had finished preaching, He said to Peter, "Now row your boat out into deeper water. Then let down your net, and you will catch a great many fish."

But Peter said, "Sir, we've been fishing all night, and we haven't caught anything. But if You say so, we'll try again."

Of course, the Lord Jesus helped Peter catch fish! When the fishermen tried to pull the net up, there were so many fish in the net that it began to rip. The men shouted for help and other fishermen rowed to them and helped them.

When Peter understood what had happened, he fell on his knees before Jesus. He knelt right there among the slippery, squirming fish.

"Leave me, Lord," said Peter, "because I am only a sinner. I am not important enough for You to even notice!"

Jesus had asked Peter, Andrew, James, and John to be His followers. But now when they realized who Jesus was, they decided to give up fishing and follow Him all the time.

Later on, Jesus saw a man who collected taxes. The man was sitting at his desk in the customs house. His name was Levi, although those who knew him well called him Matthew. Jesus said to Matthew, "Come and be one of My disciples." Immediately Matthew got up from his desk and became one of Jesus' friends.

Some days after Jesus had asked Matthew to follow Him, Jesus went off by Himself. He went up a mountain and stayed there all night talking with God. Jesus prayed all night, asking God to tell Him which men to choose as His followers.

As daylight came and the sky was turning from gray to blue, Jesus came down from the mountain. Now He was ready to choose twelve men to be His followers. Who would they be?

Jesus asked all the men who had been coming to hear Him preach, to come to a certain mountain. Jesus had already chosen five men—Peter, Andrew, James, John, and Matthew. Now with all the men gathered together, He would choose seven more men, to have twelve men who would be His special helpers.

Jesus named each one. First He named the five He had already asked to follow Him:

Peter

Andrew

James (Zebedee's son)

John

Matthew

Then He named seven more:

Philip

Bartholomew

Thomas

James (Alphaeus' son)

Thaddaeus (also called Judas)

Simon

Judas Iscariot

These twelve disciples, also called apostles, were to watch Jesus at work. They were to listen to Him preach and teach. And they were to obey Him as He taught them and helped them become His followers.

The twelve men came down from the mountain with Jesus. They stood with Him in a place where the ground was level. Many of the other people who loved Jesus stood around them. People from all over Palestine had come to hear Jesus. These people went back home after Jesus finished preaching and teaching. But the twelve men Jesus had chosen lived together, traveled together, and were Jesus' followers in a very special way.

—*Mark 1:16-20; 2:13, 14; Luke 5:1-11; 6:12-18*

Jesus Teaches by Telling Stories

Jesus had many things to teach His followers or disciples. And the twelve followers had a great deal to learn. How did Jesus teach His twelve special helpers? Sometimes Jesus told stories to help them understand new ideas, to think in new ways, and to know what God says in His Word, the Bible. Sometimes Jesus taught by showing His disciples God's power. Often Jesus asked questions to help the followers understand. And more than once Jesus asked His helpers to try teaching and preaching themselves. Then the Lord Jesus would explain how they could be better helpers and teachers.

Would you like to read some of the stories Jesus told? Can you understand them as His disciples tried to do?

A Story about Planting Seed

One day, when Jesus was staying with Peter in the town of Capernaum, Jesus went down to the Sea of Galilee. There He sat on the beach enjoying the sunshine. Soon a crowd of people gathered around Him. They asked Him to talk to them. So, as before, Jesus asked Peter to push his boat out from the shore. Then Jesus spoke to the crowd from the boat.

Perhaps as Jesus looked at the hills and fields He saw a farmer. The farmer was already at work in his field. Seeing the farmer gave Jesus an idea for a story.

"Listen," said Jesus, "once there was a farmer who went into his field to plant his seed." In Bible days farmers did not have machinery for planting seed. This farmer walked back and forth across his field as he threw the seed on the soil.

"Some of the seed," said Jesus, "fell on the path that ran between the fields of grain."

The path was hard soil because many people had walked on it, so the seed lay on the top of the ground. "Before long some birds came along," said Jesus. "They saw the seed and quickly ate it.

"Some of the seed," said Jesus, "fell on soil that was not very deep. Beneath this soil were many stones. The seed began to grow, but because there were so many stones, it could not send out strong roots. The hot sun quickly dried up the plants.

"And some of the seed fell among weeds. There was not any room for the seeds to grow. The weeds grew faster than the plants, and the plants could not grow.

"The rest of the seed," said Jesus, "fell on good ground. And here the new plant could send its roots deep into the ground. That seed grew up into strong plants. When the growing time was over, there was a good crop."

When Jesus finished His story, He said, "Anyone who has ears to hear, let him listen to My story."

Later, when Jesus was alone with His disciples, they asked Him what the story really was about. "Don't you know?" He asked. And then He explained.

The man who sows, the farmer, is like a minister or teacher who teaches the Bible. The seed stands for the Bible, God's Word. And the different kinds of soil or ground are like different kinds of people who hear the Word of God.

Some people do not listen to God's Word. They are like the path that ran between the fields. They hear God's Word, but they don't take it in. This kind of hearer hears a Bible story, but he is not really listening.

"The seed that fell on the rocky ground," said Jesus, "is like some people who hear the Word of God, but when they have problems and troubles, they forget God's Word."

Jesus told His disciples about the third kind of soil, ground with many weeds. He said that soil was like people who think many things are more important than hearing God's Word. They think having a good time, getting money, or something else is more important than listening to God's Word. Or these people have so many troubles that they worry and do not think about God.

Then Jesus told about the last part of His story. "The rest of the seed," He said, "fell on good ground. There it grew up. The good ground is like a person who gladly listens to God's Word. That person listens to the Bible and then remembers to obey what God says in His Word. That person tries to live by God's Word."

—*Mark 4:1-10, 13-20*

The Treasure

Once there was a farmer who worked some land which he did not own. The farmer rented the land from the landowner, sowed his seed, and gathered the harvest. But one day, as he was working in the field, he saw something shining in the sun. He stopped plowing and looked at the ground carefully. To his delight he found several coins.

The farmer hurried home, brought back a shovel, and dug in the place where he had found the coins. To his surprise he found many, many coins —more than he could count. Quickly he dug a deep hole and buried all of them. Then he went home and gathered together all his furniture, tools,

supplies, clothing—everything he owned. As quickly as he could, he sold everything he owned. Why? He wanted to go to the landowner and buy the field. Why was the field valuable? The farmer knew it was valuable because in the ground of that field were hundreds of coins—much more money than the field would cost.

What was Jesus teaching? Jesus said that if you have a treasure—something important to you —you will be willing to give up everything for it. Jesus said that finding out how to belong to God is like finding a treasure. He said that being a child of God is so important that a person should be willing to give up everything else.

—*Matthew 13:44*

25

A Father Shows His Love

A rich man had two sons. The younger son wanted to leave home. He wanted to do as he liked without anyone stopping him. Perhaps he was tired of obeying his father.

"Father," he said, "when you die, my brother and I will both have part of all that you own. Please give me my part now."

The father knew the boy would not use his money in the right way. But the boy kept asking, and one day the father gave in and divided his money. In a few days the younger son had packed his clothes and his share of the money and left home. He was happy as he started out. Now no one would tell him what to do!

But the father felt sorry. He watched his younger son hurry down the road. He hoped the boy would hurry home again. But he did not. And no letter came from him.

The young man did not think of his father or brother again for a long, long time. He was having a good time! He did exactly as he wanted. He bought whatever he wanted. He ate his meals where he chose. He found new friends. And his new friends helped him spend his money. They took him to places where his father would never have let him go.

One day the young man looked in his money bag. All his money was gone! Now he was poor. He knew that he had to get a job. He had not liked to work at home, and so he was not a good worker. He asked and asked, but no one would give the young man a job. His friends did not help him either. As soon as his money was gone, his friends left him. They did not want to help take care of him.

Hungry and sad, the young man finally found a job. It was not a good job. But it was the best the boy could find. What was his work? Taking care of pigs! A farmer had told the boy he could work for him. He could look after the pigs. The young man did not have enough money to buy food. Somtimes he was so hungry that he almost ate the pigs' food. No one gave him any food. No one showed him any kindness.

As the young man sat in a field watching the pigs, he thought about his father. He looked at his ragged clothes. He was hungry and unhappy. He thought, "What am I doing here? My father hires men to work for him. Those men have enough to eat. They are better off than I am. I'll go

home. I'll tell my father that I have been very, very foolish. And I have been! I have no money, no friends, and not enough to eat. I'll tell my father that I have sinned against God by being so foolish. I am not a good son. Maybe he will hire me as one of his helpers. Then I would have some clothes to wear and food to eat."

The young man got up, told the farmer he was leaving, and set off for home. Perhaps he remembered how happy he had been to leave home.

Now he was glad to go home again. He hoped his father would be glad to see him and would give him work.

The son had been gone a long time. The father may have stopped hoping that his boy would come home. But one day as the father looked down the road, he saw someone coming. Could it be? Yes, it was his son dressed in ragged clothes and looking very hungry. Quickly the father ran down the road to the boy. He put his

27

arms around the young man.

"Oh, Father," said the boy, "I have sinned against God. I should not even be called your son anymore."

But before the son could finish speaking, the father stopped him by calling to the servants. "Bring some new clothing for my son. Fix some good food. The boy I thought was gone forever is home!"

Now the older son had not left home. He had worked hard. When he heard that his father was getting a big dinner ready for his brother, he was angry. In fact, he was so very angry that he would not go into the house.

When the father heard how his older boy felt, he went to him. "Son," he said, "what is the trouble? What is bothering you?"

"Look," said the older son, "I have worked for you for many years. I have always tried to obey you. But you have never made a big dinner for me. My brother has not obeyed you! He has spent his money foolishly. But you are making a big fuss over him. It's just not fair!"

Then the father put his arms around this son. "Look, boy," he said, "I know what a good son you have been. I love you very much. You know that everything I have is yours. You can do anything you want. Have a big dinner, if you want, and invite your friends. But it's different with your brother. He was glad to leave us. I thought he would not come home again. Now he is here, and I cannot help being happy. I thought he was dead, but he's alive. Come, be happy with me!"

—*Luke 15:11-32*

Ten Young Women

The disciples knew that Jesus was going to die. But they also knew that sometime Jesus would come back to Earth. He wanted His followers to be ready for Him when He came.

Jesus said, "The coming of the Lord in His kingdom will be something like a wedding." Of course, Jesus was talking about a Bible-time wedding. The wedding He told about was at night.

Sometimes the bride's relatives would take her to the bridegroom's house. But more often the bridegroom would come to the bride's house to take her to his home.

When the bridegroom and bride left her house, many people would follow. But there was one rule. To be in the parade following the bride and bridegroom, every person had to have a Bible-time lamp that burned oil.

"Ten young women were waiting at the bride's house for the bridegroom," said Jesus. "Five of them had brought some extra oil for their lamps. Five of them forgot to bring extra oil.

"The bridegroom, the young man who was to be married, was late in coming. While they were waiting for him, the ten young women fell asleep. At midnight there was a shout, 'Here is the bridegroom! Go out to meet him!'

"The five girls who had brought extra oil put it in their lamps. They were ready. But the five girls who had not brought extra oil were not ready. They had burned up all the oil they had put in their lamps. 'Give us some oil, please,' they said to the other girls. But those girls said, 'We're sorry, but we don't have enough for ourselves and for you. Go buy some oil.'

"The five girls who needed oil hurried off to buy it. But while they were gone, all of the wedding party followed the bridegroom to his house.

"After a time, the five girls came to the house. 'Oh, sir, please open the door,' they called. But the bridegroom would not open the door."

Jesus said, "You be ready for Me to come again. Keep watching for Me because you don't know when I will come."

—*Matthew 25:1-13*

The Good Samaritan

One day, as Jesus was preaching to the people, a lawyer stood up to ask Jesus a question. He said, "What must I do to have eternal life?"

Jesus asked him, "What do you read in the Scriptures?" The lawyer said, "You are to love God as much as possible, and love your neighbor as yourself."

"Then do it," said Jesus. But the young man was not content with the answer. He asked, "But who is my neighbor?"

Jesus gave the lawyer his answer by telling a story. In Bible times the Jews did not think everyone was important. In fact, they seemed to think that only Jews were important. They hated the people who lived in the country of Samaria, who were called Samaritans.

One day a man was traveling from the city of Jerusalem to the city of Jericho. His way was along a very lonely road. On each side of the road were many stones and big rocks. The man knew that robbers often hid behind the big rocks. They would rush out to grab money or anything else from people traveling along the road.

Suddenly some robbers did run out on the road. They hit the man and took his money. Then they ran away leaving the man by the side of the road.

After a long, long time the man heard footsteps coming along the road. By moving his head a little the man could see the person coming. He was a minister-priest from the Temple in Jerusalem. Surely he would help the wounded man.

But the minister-priest did not even stop. He quickly walked along the other side of the road. Yes, he walked right past the hurt man.

"Will no one come to help me?" he must have thought. As he wondered, he heard more footsteps coming. Perhaps he called, "Help!" But

the second man did not stop either. He, too, was a Jew and a helper at the Temple.

Poor, helpless, dying man! There seemed to be no one who would help him. Perhaps he thought of his wife and children at home. Perhaps he prayed for help. Then, just as he felt very much alone, he heard a noise.

It was the sound of donkey hoofs pounding on the road. The sound came closer, till it stopped. The wounded man tried to raise his head to see. And he looked right into the face of someone bending over him. Who was it? Not another Jew, but a man from Samaria, a Samaritan.

"You poor man," said the Samaritan. "Let me help you. I'll try to wash your cuts with some oil. And I have some cloth to use for bandages."

After the Samaritan put bandages over the cuts, he helped the man get on his own donkey. Carefully the Samaritan put his arm around the wounded man. The Samaritan guided the donkey around rough places in the road. He was taking the man to an inn that was halfway between Jerusalem and Jericho.

When the two men reached the inn, the Samaritan helped the innkeeper take care of the wounded man. The next day the Samaritan had to go on his way. But before he left he said to the innkeeper, "Take care of the man. Here is some money. If you need more than this, I will pay you the next time I stop."

After Jesus finished the story, He asked the lawyer a question. "Tell Me," He said, "which of the three men would you say was a neighbor of the man who was beaten?"

The lawyer hated to say, "The Samaritan." Instead the lawyer said, "The one who was kind."

"All right," Jesus said, "You go and do what you can for everyone who needs your help."

—Luke 10:25-37

31

The Workmen in the Vineyard

Perhaps Jesus' disciples wondered if they were the only ones who would tell others about Him. If other people were to tell about Jesus, would they get more honor than the disciples? Jesus told a story to help answer their questions.

"One day the owner of a vineyard went to town early in the morning. He wanted to hire workmen to gather grapes.

"The owner said to some men looking for work, 'If you work in my vineyard today, I will pay you $20.' And the men went to work.

"About nine o'clock in the morning the owner of the vineyard hired more workers. By noon he could see that he still needed more men. He went to town and hired some more workers. He did the same thing at three o'clock in the afternoon.

"At five o'clock in the afternoon he went to town again. He saw some men standing around. He said, 'Why have you been waiting around all day?' They said, 'Because no one has hired us.' The owner said, 'Go out to my vineyard and work there.'

"That evening all the workers were being paid.

Everyone was paid the same amount. The workers who had worked from early morning were angry. 'Look,' they said, 'why should we get only the same amount of money as the workers who began at five o'clock?'

" 'Friends,' said the owner, 'I have done nothing wrong. You agreed to work all day for what I offered you. Take the money and go. Should you be angry because I am kind to the men who began work later than you did?' "

"The last shall be first," Jesus said, "and the first, last."

The disciples must have wondered about this story. Perhaps they thought that the men who worked twelve hours should have received twelve times as much as the men who worked one hour.

What did Jesus want His friends to learn from this story? He wanted them to think about all God does for His children. Can God's children possibly earn all that God gives them? No, of course not. Jesus was trying to have His disciples see that men pay only for work that is done. But God gives to everyone who is willing to work for Him.

—Matthew 20:1-16

The Trusted Servants

Jesus had told the disciples that He was going to die. He also told them that one day He would come back to Earth. He wanted His followers to be ready for Him.

"Once there was a man who owned a great amount of land," Jesus said. "Before the man left on a trip he gave orders to some of his servants. He loaned his servants some money. Then he told them to invest the money for him while he was gone.

"To one servant the rich man gave ten thousand dollars. To another one he gave four thousand dollars. And he gave the third servant two thousand dollars. Then he went away.

"Right after the man left, the first two servants began to work. They bought things with the money and then sold what they had bought for a higher price. Soon the servant who had ten thousand dollars had twenty thousand. The servant who had four thousand dollars had eight thousand dollars. But the third servant, to whom had been given two

thousand dollars, did nothing. He took the money dug a hole in the ground, and very carefully buried it.

"After a long time the rich man came home. He called his servants together to find out what they had done. The first servant came with bags of money. 'Look,' he said, 'I have twice as much money for you now.'

" 'Well done!' said the rich man. 'I trusted you with ten thousand dollars. Now I will trust you with much more.'

"The second servant came with bags of money. 'Look,' he said, 'you gave me four thousand dollars, and I have worked to make it eight thousand dollars.'

" 'Good,' said the rich man. 'I trusted you with a small amount of money. Now I will trust you with larger amounts of money.'

"Last of all came the third servant. He was carrying the very same bag of money that the rich man had given him. 'Look,' he said, 'I was afraid to try buying and selling with your money. I was afraid of losing your money, so I did nothing. I dug a hole in the ground and buried your money. Here it is, just as you gave it to me!'

"But the rich man was not pleased. He said, 'You are no good! You know that I am a good businessman. Why didn't you use my money to make more money? Even if you were afraid to buy and sell, you could have loaned my money to someone. That person could have paid interest on my money. At least you could have made a little money. Now because you haven't done anything with the money, I'm giving it to someone else.' And the rich man gave the bag of money to his first servant."

This story helped Jesus' friends to understand what they should do while He was away. He was telling them to use whatever they had—money, knowledge, or abilities—for God. Jesus was saying that whoever does not use what he has will surely lose it.

—*Matthew 25:14-30*

A Story about Thistles

The Lord Jesus told His friends a story about a farmer that sowed the best seed he could find. Of course he expected a good crop. One night the farmer's enemy came and planted thistle seeds all over the field. Then the enemy crept away as quietly as he had come.

When the wheat began to grow, the prickly thistle plants grew too. The farmer's men saw what was happening. They said, "Surely, sir, you planted good seed in your field, didn't you? Well, there are a lot of thistles growing in the field now. How do you suppose that happened?"

The farmer was very angry. "I know what has happened," he said. "I have an enemy who wants me to have a poor crop. He has planted thistle seeds in my field."

Then the farmer's workers asked, "Do you want us to weed the field now?"

"Let the thistles and the wheat grow," the farmer said, "till it's time for the harvest. Then I will tell the workers to cut the grain, gather the thistles together, and tie them into bundles. We'll burn the thistles, but the workers can gather the wheat and store it in my barn."

"What does this story mean?" the disciples asked each other. Then Jesus explained.

"I am like the farmer. The good seed stands for the people who love God. But everyone does not love God. The people who do not love Him are like the thistles. Can you see that people who love God and those who do not love Him are living together in this world?

"But someday it will be different. The Lord will send His angels to gather together all the people who do not love Him and who do not believe in Him. Then He will destroy those people just as the thistles were burned. But the people who love the Lord will shine as the sun. Let those who have ears listen to My words and believe them."

—Matthew 13:24-30, 37-43

SoJ—C¹

A Story Told at Dinner

One time Jesus was invited to dinner at the home of a Pharisee. Pharisees were men who belonged to an important religious and political group. They were proud to be known as Pharisees.

After dinner, Jesus began to talk. He had noticed that when the guests came to the dinner, some had wanted the best places. The best place was thought to be nearest the one giving the dinner. Some men had chosen their places at the table without waiting to be told which was theirs. Jesus wanted everyone to think more of others than of himself.

"If you are invited to a feast," Jesus said, "don't always try to get the best seat. You may get into trouble. Suppose you do get the best seat, will you keep it? No, not if someone shows up who deserves it more than you do. The one giving the dinner may say to you, 'Please move. Let this man sit here.' You'll feel foolish then! You'll have to take a seat at the other end of the table.

"Do this when you go to a party. Take the seat at the end of the table. Then the one giving the party may say, 'Friend, I have a better place than this for you.' If he does, you will be made to feel important in front of everyone else. For everyone who thinks too much of himself will be made to feel very unimportant."

Then Jesus turned to the man giving the dinner. He had some advice for this man too. "When you give a party," said Jesus, "don't invite friends, brothers, relatives, and rich neighbors. They will return your invitation. Instead, invite the poor,

the crippled, the lame, and the blind. Then God will reward you for inviting those who cannot take their turn in giving big dinner parties."

Perhaps the Pharisees who heard all this thought themselves to be most important to God. Jesus told a story to help them see that all who love God are important to Him.

"One time a man sent out invitations to a party," said Jesus. "When all the food was ready, the man sent a servant to remind the guests of the dinner party. But every guest made an excuse for not coming. One said he had just bought some land and wanted to go see it. Another one said he had bought some oxen and wanted to try the animals out. Another guest said he had just been married and could not come.

"When the servant came back with the news that no one was coming, the man was angry. 'Go to the streets in the city,' he said. 'Find anyone who can come. Invite poor people. Bring people who are crippled, lame, or blind.'

"The servant did as he was told. But even after some people came, there was still room. 'Now go out in the country. Find anyone who can come. I want my house to be filled,' said the man. And the servant obeyed."

What did Jesus mean by this story? The Pharisees had known about God for a long time. Perhaps they thought that they were the only people important to God. The story would help them see that God loves everyone!

—*Luke 14:7-24*

The Rich Man and the Poor Man

This is a story that Jesus told His disciples. It is a story about people who love money and a good time instead of obeying God.

There was once a rich man who had everything that he wanted. The rich man dressed up in purple clothes everyday. Kings wore purple clothing, and this man wanted to dress as a king would dress. Not only did the rich man have good clothes, but everyday he had delicious meals. In fact he always had more food than he could possibly eat. The rich man had everything that he wanted.

One day a stranger appeared at the rich man's door. The stranger, whose name was Lazarus, was very poor. Lazarus was in rags and never had enough to eat. Someone had brought him to the rich man's house and left him there. His body was covered with sores that would not heal. He could not work. Probably Lazarus thought that the rich man who had so much would give him some bits of leftover food. Lazarus was so weak and helpless that when dogs came and licked his sores he was not strong enough to make them go away.

Did the rich man give Lazarus food or clothing? No, he did not! Finally Lazarus died. Angels came for Lazarus and took him to be with Abraham and other people in the special place God had planned for people who love Him.

Sometime later the rich man died. Angels did

not take the rich man to Abraham. The rich man found himself in Hades, the place God sends those who do not love Him.

The rich man was in pain in the world of the dead who do not love God. He looked up and could see Lazarus a long way off. Lazarus looked very well. The rich man cried out to Abraham, "Father Abraham, please help me. Send Lazarus here to dip his finger in water and cool my tongue. It is very painful here in this fire! Please help me!"

Then Abraham said to the rich man, "My son, do not forget that when you were living in the world you had many good things. Lazarus had only bad things. Now he is well cared for, but you are in pain. Lazarus can't come to you. There is a big deep canyon or valley between us. No one from here can come to you, and you cannot come to us."

"Oh," groaned the rich man. "Then I ask you to send Lazarus back to Earth to my family. I have five brothers. Let Lazarus talk to them, or they will have to come to this terrible place too."

But Abraham said to him, "Your brothers already have the writings of Moses and the prophets. Let them pay attention to that part of God's Word."

"No, Father Abraham," said the rich man, "if someone goes to them from the dead, they will be sorry for their sins and turn from them."

Then Abraham said, "If your brothers do not believe what Moses wrote, they will not listen even if someone is sent to them from the dead. They will not change their ways."

—Luke 16:19-31

The House on the Sand

The Lord Jesus and His disciples had been together all day. Up on the mountain the disciples had talked with Jesus. They had listened to all He had said. Now it was time to go down from the mountain.

Who was waiting for Jesus at the bottom of the mountain? Many, many people who wanted to touch Jesus. They knew that He could make them well and strong. And Jesus, the Son of God, did make them well. But He did more than that! He told them how to obey God. Jesus said it is very important to obey the Lord.

"If you listen to Me," Jesus said, "and try to please the Lord, you are very wise. But if you listen to Me and do not remember to do the things I tell you, you are very foolish. A story will help you understand.

"Two men planned to build houses," Jesus told the listening people. "One man dug deep into the ground until his shovel hit rock. He knew that a house built on rock would last for a long time.

"But the second man did not bother to dig down to rocky ground. He decided to build his house on top of the sandy soil, which was not strong and firm like rock."

After the two houses were finished, the rains fell and strong winds blew. The river had so much water in it that the water came over the banks and rushed against the two houses.

What happened? The house built on rock was not damaged. That house was just as strong as it had ever been. But the house built on sand crumbled and fell with a huge crash. The wreck of that house was terrible!

Jesus said, "People who hear what God wants them to do and do it are wise. But people who listen to My words and don't obey the Lord, are like the foolish man who built his house on the sand and his house fell."

—*Luke 6:46-49*

Jesus Tells about the End of the World

Once Jesus told about the time when He will come back in great glory. He will sit on His throne. Angels will be around Him. All the nations of the world will be gathered together before Him. Then Jesus will pass judgment on each and every one. He will be like a shepherd gathering the sheep on one side and the goats on the other. He will tell people who obeyed Him to come to His right side. He will tell people who did not love and obey Him to stand at His left.

Then Jesus will say, "Come, you who love Me. You have My Father's blessing. Come, join with Me in the kingdom made for you. When I was hungry, you fed Me. When I was thirsty, you gave Me water. When I was a stranger, you invited Me into your homes. You gave Me clothing when I needed it. You visited Me in prison."

The people on the right will ask, "Lord, when did we see You in need

and do this for You?"

And Jesus will say, "Whenever you helped someone, you were helping Me."

Then Jesus will turn to those on His left. He will say, "Get out of My sight! You are being sent to the eternal fire prepared for the devil and his demons. When I was hungry, you would not feed Me. When I was thirsty, you would not give Me a drink. When I was a stranger, you would not do anything for Me."

The people will say, "Lord when did we see You hungry or thirsty or sick or in prison, and not help You?"

Jesus will say, "When you did not give to people who needed your help, it was the same as though you were treating Me the same way. When you would not help others, you were not helping Me."

Then all those who did not love the Lord and help others will be punished. They will be sent away. But the people who loved the Lord and obeyed Him will live with Him forever.

—*Matthew 25:31-46*

Jesus Heals Many People

While Jesus was here on Earth, He made many people well again. He healed the lame, the blind, and the deaf. The Bible has reports about some of the work Jesus did.

The Man Who Could Not Walk

"Oh, I am so tired of being sick. My arms won't move. My legs won't walk. I feel terrible!"

The unhappy man who felt so bad lay on his mat with his eyes shut. He had been sick for a long, long time. But being sick was not the only thing that bothered him. He kept thinking about all of the bad things he had done. He remembered the bad words he had said. He remembered telling lies. How much he must have wished that he could forget his sin. Was there anyone who could help him?

Yes, in his very town was a Man who could help him. Jesus was teaching and healing in his town. Now the sick man probably did not know about Jesus, but he had four friends who did. The friends came hurrying to the sick man with the good news.

Perhaps one friend said, "Listen! Jesus is here. Right here in our town! He can make you walk again. Let's take you to Him."

The four friends took hold of the man's mat. Quickly they walked down the street to the house where Jesus was. But the house was filled with people. The street was crowded with people. There seemed to be no way to get their friend to Jesus.

Then they thought of a way. The friends climbed the outside stairway to the roof. They put the mat down and began taking up part of the roof. The roof of the Bible-time house was made of sand and dry hard mud, with some strips of wood laid across the beams. Soon the men had made a hole in the roof. Then they fastened ropes to each corner of the sick man's mat and let him down through the hole.

Of course, Jesus stopped teaching when the mat began coming down. Jesus looked at the man and saw that he could not move. But Jesus knew there was something that the man needed more than being made well. He knew how the man felt because of all his wrongdoing. Jesus said, "Son, your sins are forgiven."

The sick man did not say, "Jesus, I would rather walk than have my sins forgiven." No, he was so happy to know that he had been forgiven, that he could not think of anything else.

But some Jewish rulers, standing close by, were not happy to hear what Jesus said. They did not believe that Jesus is God's Son. They did not want to believe that He had power to forgive sins.

Jesus could read their minds. He said, "Why does it bother you for Me to forgive this man? Is it any harder to forgive his sins than to heal him? But to prove that I have power to forgive sin, I will heal him, too."

Then Jesus said to the man, "You are well. Pick up your bed and go home!"

The man jumped up, took his bed, and pushed through the crowd of people to the door. All the people said, "We never saw anything like this before!"

—Mark 2:1-12

Jesus Calms the Sea and Heals a Wild Man

The Sea of Galilee was a good place to fish. Men fished there at night. During the day they cleaned and mended their nets. But on one special day the men were not busy with their nets. The beach was crowded with people who had all come to see Jesus.

Jesus spent all day teaching the people. He was tired when evening came, so He said to His disciples, "Let's go over to the other side of the lake." They started out, leaving the crowd of people behind.

But soon a terrible storm began. The waves became higher and higher. Soon the waves were so high that water splashed into the boat until it was nearly full of water. Then the boat began to sink.

Jesus was tired when He got into the boat. He went to the back of the boat where He could lay down. There He fell asleep. The fishermen must have been out on the lake in other storms. But now no matter how hard they rowed, they could not bring the boat to land. They became frightened. Would they drown?

Jesus still slept quietly in the boat. Then one of the men shook Him hard enough to wake Him. "Teacher," he asked, "don't you care that we are going to drown?"

Jesus got up at once. He did not touch the oars. He did not tell the men to bail out the water. He spoke quietly to the splashing stormy water. He said, "Quiet down!" And right away the wind stopped and the water was quiet. Then Jesus asked, "Why were you afraid? Don't you trust Me yet?"

The disciples looked at each other. They said, "Even the wind and the sea obey this Man."

After the storm stopped, Jesus and His disciples went on across the lake to the other side. When they stepped out of the boat and onto the shore, a wild man came running out from a cemetery. The wild man lived in the cemetery. He was so strong that he could rip handcuffs off. There was no chain that he could not tear. There was no doctor to help him and no place to keep him. Day and night the man walked about the cemetery, crying and cutting himself with sharp stones.

When the wild man saw Jesus, he ran to Him. He knelt before Jesus. Then Jesus spoke to the evil spirit that was living in the man and making him act as he did. "Come out, you evil spirit," said Jesus.

The evil spirit, or demon, called out, "What do I have to do with you, Jesus, Son of the most high God? Please do not hurt me."

Jesus asked, "What is your name?" Then the evil spirit replied, "Legion, for there are many of us here inside this man."

Now there was a big herd of pigs, about two thousand, near the cemetery. Seeing the pigs, the evil spirits said, "Send us into those pigs!"

So Jesus told the evil spirits that they could go into the pigs. Then the evil spirits left the man and entered into the pigs. Right away the pigs ran down the hill and into the lake. The men who were taking care of the pigs were afraid. They hurried off to the town to tell everyone what had happened.

Before long a crowd of people who had heard what had happened came to Jesus. They saw the wild man sitting quietly. Now he was able to talk with them because he behaved like any other man. He wasn't wild anymore.

When the people saw that the man was well, they were afraid. They were afraid of Jesus' power. They asked Him to please go away and leave them alone.

One person was not afraid of Jesus. It was the man who had been made well. When Jesus got back into the boat, the man asked to go along. "No," said Jesus, "you go home to your friends. Tell them what a great thing God has done for you."

The man went off to his home and friends. He went from city to city, telling people what Jesus had done for him.

—Mark 4:35—5:20

SoJ—D

A Roman Captain Has Faith in Jesus

"Jesus is coming! Jesus is coming!" This news reached the city of Capernaum long before Jesus and His disciples got there. Jesus' friends were glad to hear this news. Other people were glad to hear it too. They wanted to see Jesus and talk with Him. Perhaps many of them hoped that He would make them well.

One person who wanted to see Jesus was a captain in the Roman army. He was in charge of a hundred soldiers who lived in a fort near the city. The Roman captain was a friend of the Jewish people. He had built a synagogue for them.

The captain had a servant, one of his slaves. Now the slave was very ill. The captain felt sure that the slave was going to die unless someone could help him. When the captain knew that Jesus was coming, he thought of his sick slave. Surely Jesus could cure the man.

But the captain did not go to see Jesus himself. Perhaps he thought it would do better if some of the Jewish rulers talked to Jesus. Of course, the Jewish rulers were glad to help the man who had been kind to them. So they went to Jesus and told Him about the captain and his dying slave. They said that the captain was asking Jesus to help the sick man. Then they told Jesus about the captain. "He is a good man," they said. "He loves our people. Why, he has even built a synagogue for us. If anyone deserves Your help, this man does. Please come with us to see him."

Jesus went with the men. But before they got to the captain's home, some men came to meet them. The men were servants sent by the captain. "Lord," said the servant who had a message from the captain, "don't bother to come to my home.

I am not good enough to have You come to me," said the servant as he repeated the captain's message. "If You will just speak a word from where You are, I know that my servant will be well again. I know that You can heal him. I am in charge of one hundred soldiers. When I command my soldiers, they obey me. I know that You have power to command sickness to leave. You have power to make anyone well. So just say, 'Be well!' and the sickness will leave my servant."

When Jesus heard this message, He was pleased. He knew that the captain really trusted Him. He turned to the Jewish rulers who were with Him. "Look," He said, "I have never found a man in Israel with faith like this captain has!"

And when the captain's men got back home, the servant was well!

—Luke 7:1-10

Jesus Feeds Hungry People

More and more people heard about Jesus' wonderful power to heal the sick. Of course, great crowds of people came to Him. So many people that Jesus and His disciples could not find any time or place to rest.

One day Jesus and His disciples got into a boat. Perhaps if they crossed the lake they would find a place where they could be alone. But as soon as people saw where Jesus was going, they followed Him. Hundreds of people walked along the shore of the lake until they came to the place where Jesus and His friends were resting.

When Jesus saw all the people coming, He did not say "Go away!" No, Jesus never says, "Go away!" to anyone. Jesus looked at the people and felt sorry for them. He had climbed part way up a hill by the side of the lake. Here all the people could see Him as he began to teach. He talked to the people about God and His plan for them. There were sick people in the crowd, and Jesus healed them.

Jesus talked all day with the people. Then, as it was getting toward evening, the disciples came to Him. "Master," they said, "send the people away. It is getting late, and there is nothing here for them to eat."

But Jesus said, "You feed them!"

How surprised the disciples were to hear His words. How could they feed the people? One of the disciples said, "We don't have enough money to buy food." Then Andrew spoke up, "There's a boy here who has five small rolls and a couple of fish. But what good are they with all this crowd?"

"Tell everyone to sit down," said Jesus. All the people sat down as the boy came to Jesus with the lunch he had brought from home. When everyone was seated, Jesus took the bread and the fish. He gave thanks to God and then passed pieces of bread to the disciples to give to the people. He did the same with the fish. What happened? There was enough bread and fish for everyone to have all he could eat!

When the people had finished their meal, Jesus told His disciples to gather up all the pieces that were left. He did not want any food wasted. His disciples gathered up enough bread and fish to fill twelve baskets. Jesus had fed more than five thousand people from five rolls and two fish. When the people saw what Jesus had done, they said, "Surely this Man is the One we have been looking for!"

The people were so excited about Jesus' great power that they wanted to make Him King. When Jesus saw what they wanted to do, He slipped away into the hills where they could not find Him. After it got dark, Jesus and His disciples got into the boat and went back across the lake.

The next day the people looked for Jesus. When

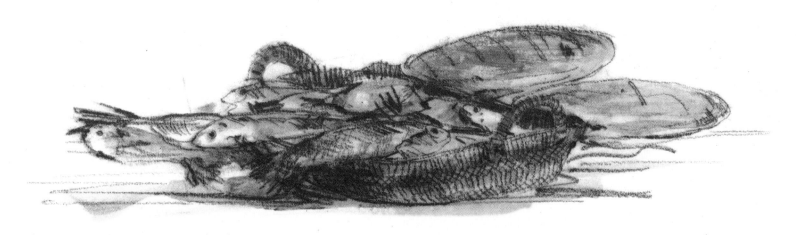

they saw that the boat was gone, they hurried to the other side where Jesus was. They said to Him, Him, "Teacher, when did You come here from across the lake?"

Jesus knew why they were looking for Him. "Look," He said, "you want to be with Me because I fed you. You are not looking for Me because you believe I am God's Son. Really, you should not think that bread is so important. Spend your time looking for the eternal life that I can give you. God sent Me for this very purpose."

"What should we do to satisfy God?" they asked.

Jesus told them, "This is the will of God, that you believe in Me because He has sent Me. Everyone who really believes in Me as God's Son shall have eternal life."

—*John 6:1-29*

Jesus in Jerusalem

The city of Jerusalem was the capital of Palestine in Bible times. In this city was the beautiful Temple. Jewish people from all over the country made trips to the Temple to worship. Jesus, too, planned to worship in Jerusalem before He died on the cross.

On the way to Jerusalem, Jesus and His disciples went through the town of Jericho. In Jericho lived a rich man named Zacchaeus. Zacchaeus was a tax collector who had cheated in his work. He had taken money that was not his. When Zacchaeus heard that Jesus was coming to Jericho, he wanted to see Him.

Zacchaeus joined the crowd of people that lined both sides of the road. But he was too short to see over the heads of the people. Suddenly he had an idea. Down the road he ran till he came to a tree with low branches. Quickly Zacchaeus grabbed a branch and climbed up into the tree.

Soon Jesus and His friends came down the road. When they reached the tree where Zacchaeus was, Jesus stopped, looked up, and said, "Zacchaeus, hurry down. I am going to visit your house today."

Zacchaeus was surprised! How did Jesus know his name? He scrambled down and took Jesus to his home. After listening to Jesus, Zacchaeus thought differently. He wanted to be honest. He said, "Look, Lord, I've done wrong, but now I

will give half of all I own to the poor. And if I have taken more from any man than I should have, I will give him back four times as much as I took."

Jesus must have been pleased as He looked at Zacchaeus and said, "What you say shows that salvation has come to your house. The Son of Man has come to seek and save people like you."

After leaving Zacchaeus, Jesus again told His friends what was going to happen to Him in Jerusalem. "When we get there," Jesus said, "I am going to be arrested. I will have to stand trial before some of the Jewish rulers. They are going to find Me guilty of saying that I am God's Son.

You know that I am the Son of God, but many people do not think I am. They will beat Me. Finally, they will put Me to death, but I am going to come back to life!"

The disciples could not understand all that Jesus said. They were afraid, but they probably thought that the rulers could not harm their powerful Leader. Jesus knew what they were thinking. He said, "I came to give My life for other people. I came to be the Saviour of all who believe in Me."

Blind Bartimaeus

As Jesus and His friends walked along the road from Jericho to Jerusalem, there were many people who wanted to see Him. But one man had to sit by the highway, hoping that Jesus would see him.

This man, blind Bartimaeus, sat by the side of the road asking people for money. He heard the footsteps of many people hurrying past. "What's happening?" he asked. When someone shouted to him, "Jesus is coming!" blind Bartimaeus was glad. He shouted with all his strength, "Jesus, Son of David, have pity on me! Help me!"

When Jesus heard what Bartimaeus was saying, He stopped. "Someone bring Bartimaeus here," commanded Jesus. A man ran to Bartimaeus. "You are lucky," he said. "Jesus wants to see you."

Bartimaeus was excited! He ran to Jesus. "What do you want Me to do for you?" asked Jesus.

"Oh," said Bartimaeus, "I want to see!"

And Jesus said, "All right, because you believe in Me, you shall see." Right then Bartimaeus could see. How happy he was as he followed Jesus and His friends down the road.

—*Mark 10:32-34, 45-52; Luke 19:1-10*

Jesus Enters the City

As Jesus and His disciples came to another town near Jerusalem, He asked His disciples to do something for Him. "Go into the town that is just ahead of us," Jesus told two of His disciples. "Just as you get into the town, you'll see a colt tied near a house.

The colt has never been ridden. Bring him to Me."

Perhaps the disciples wondered if anyone would get after them for taking a colt. Jesus must have known their thoughts, for He said, "If anyone asks you what you are doing, just say, 'Our Master needs him. We'll bring him back again.'"

The disciples went off to obey. They found the colt and untied it. And some men did say, "What are you doing? That animal is not yours!" Then the disciples answered just as Jesus had told them to do. And the men agreed to let the colt go.

The disciples brought the colt to Jesus, and some of the other disciples put their coats over its back. The colt would be easier to ride this way. Then Jesus climbed on the colt.

When the crowd saw what Jesus was doing, they began to spread their coats on the road. They wanted Jesus to ride into the city as a king would

do. Some people cut branches from trees and waved them.

"Long live the King!" they cried. "Hosanna in the highest! Blessed is He who comes in the name of the Lord! Hosanna! Hosanna!"

And in this way Jesus came into Jerusalem. He went to the Temple and looked at everything in it. Then as evening came, He went back to the town of Bethany with His twelve disciples.

—Mark 11:1-11

Jesus in the Temple

The next day, Jesus and His disciples returned to the Temple. The Temple was supposed to be a very holy place where people came to make sacrifices to God. But when Jesus and His disciples reached the Temple, they found that it looked more like a market than a place to worship God. All around were cattle and sheep. The men who owned the animals shouted to the people as they came along. Each man wanted people to buy his animals. There were also cages filled with pigeons and doves. The frightened birds flew about their cages, chirping wildly to be let loose. And there was still another noise—the clink of money being dropped on a table as people traded money used in other lands for the money used in Jerusalem. The money changers, as the men at the table were called, tried to cheat people whenever they could.

Just the day before, crowds of people had welcomed Jesus to Jerusalem. But the men in the Temple were not glad to see Him. They knew they were doing wrong. Now, suddenly, Jesus knocked

over the tables of the money changers. He opened the birds' cages, and the pens where the animals were kept. Jesus chased the money changers and the men who owned the animals right out of the Temple. He said, "Don't you know it is written in the Scripture, 'My Temple is to be a place of prayer for all nations'? You have changed it into a place where people are robbed!"

Of course, when the Jewish rulers saw what was happening, they were angry. They began to plan how they would get rid of Jesus. But they knew many of the people liked Jesus. How could they get rid of Him without causing the people to start a riot?

—Mark 11:15-18

The Rulers Have a Plan

Jesus knew what the rulers were planning. He said to His disciples, "You know that the Passover celebration begins in two days. Soon I shall be betrayed and killed."

At that very time some of the Jewish rulers and chief priests were meeting to plan how to capture Jesus. How could they? They needed to take Jesus when He was alone, not when crowds were about Him.

Now, one disciple was very different from the others. He did not believe what Jesus was teaching. And he did not like it because he was not making money as a disciple. His name was Judas Iscariot, and he decided to help the rulers capture Jesus.

Judas went to the chief priests and said, "What will you give me if I help you get Jesus?" The rulers and priests gladly gave Judas thirty pieces of silver. And from that time on Judas watched for a chance to help the rulers take Jesus.

—Matthew 26:1-5, 14-16

Jesus Eats Supper with His Disciples

The day for the Passover feast came. Jesus told Peter and John to get things ready. "Where shall we have our feast?" they asked.

Jesus said, "Look for a man carrying a jar of water. Follow him. Then say to the owner of the house to which he leads you that the Master has sent you. Tell him that you want to see the room where we are going to eat our Passover supper. He will take you upstairs to a large room. Prepare our supper there." Peter and John obeyed, and they found everything as He had said it would be.

In the evening Jesus came with the other disciples. Jesus was sad because He knew that this would be His last supper with the disciples. Perhaps the disciples themselves were wondering if Jesus really would be taken from them.

As the disciples and Jesus were eating, He said, "One of you here is going to give Me over to My enemies." Each disciple said, "Lord, am I the one?"

Jesus said, "Yes, one of you will give Me away. It would be better for that man if he had never been born."

Then Judas pretended that he was not the one. He asked, "Master, is it I?" And Jesus said, "Yes."

As they were eating, Jesus took a small loaf of bread. He asked God's blessing on it and then said, "Take this bread and eat it, for it is My body which is broken for you." Then Jesus took a cup. "Drink all of you from this cup. It is My blood which is poured out for many for the forgiveness of sins."

After saying these things, Jesus got up from the table. In Bible times, people did something special for their guests. Since everyone wore open sandals, their feet got dusty and tired. So, when a guest arrived at a house, someone would pour water over the guest's feet. Then he would wipe them dry. But Peter and John seemed to have forgotten this custom. So Jesus now took off His long robe, wrapped a towel around His waist, and poured water into a large pan. Then He began to wash the disciples' feet. He wiped them with the towel.

Jesus said, "Look, Peter, you don't understand now why I am doing this, but you will someday."

"No," said Peter, "You shall not wash my feet."

"But if I don't," said Jesus, "you can't be one of My helpers."

"Oh," said Peter, "then wash my hands and my head. I want to be Your helper."

After washing the men's feet, Jesus put His robe on again. "You call Me Master and Lord," He said, "That is right, for I am Lord. But if I, the Lord, wash your feet, you should wash each other's feet. I have given you an example. Do as I have done to you."

—Matthew 26:17-18; Mark 14:13-16; John 13:1-15

Jesus is Captured and Killed

Jesus and His disciples were going to the Garden of Gethsemane. Jesus and His disciples had probably been in the garden before. But tonight was different. There was something terrible about it. Jesus knew that He would die on the next day.

"Look," said Jesus, "all of you are going to leave Me alone tonight. But after I have died, I'll come back to life again and see you."

Before anyone else could speak, Peter said, "Lord, even if everyone else leaves You, I won't!"

Jesus looked at Peter. He said, "Yes, before the rooster crows tomorrow morning, you will say three times that you do not know Me."

Again Peter and the other disciples promised

not to leave Jesus. Just then Jesus and His friends reached the garden.

Three of the disciples—Peter, James, and John—walked on into the garden with Jesus. But Jesus wanted to be all alone when He talked to God, so He told the three men to sit a little distance away from Him and pray too.

Jesus was not afraid to die. But He could hardly stand to think of the terrible burden of sin that He would carry on the cross. He knew that He would be carrying the sin of every single person. What a terrible load to carry or bear! He knew, too, that when God looked at Him, God would see Jesus as a Sin-bearer, not as His own Son. God would not be treating Him as His Son, but as a sinner. No wonder Jesus wanted to talk to His Father before this terrible thing happened.

Jesus threw Himself down on the ground and began to pray. "My Father," Jesus called out, "if it is possible, let this cup pass from Me. But Your will be done."

When Jesus said "cup," He was thinking of all the terrible things that were going to happen to Him. Because Jesus is God's Son, He knew exactly all that would take place.

Then Jesus went to His three disciples and found them asleep. "Peter," He called, "can't you stay awake for even an hour?"

Again Jesus went back to pray. "Oh, Father!" He prayed, "if this cup cannot go away, Your will be done."

Again Jesus found the disciples asleep. He prayed one more time, and found the disciples still asleep. Then He said, "All right, sleep on! The

time will soon be here when I shall be betrayed into the hands of evil men."

At that very moment, Judas and a mob of people and soldiers with swords and clubs came into the garden. Judas and the soldiers had been sent by the chief priests. Judas had said to the mob, "Now watch. Grab the Man I greet."

Judas walked over to Jesus. He said, "Hello, Master!" Then he kissed Jesus on the cheek. Jesus said, "My friend, I know why you are here. Go ahead and take Me."

When Jesus' disciples saw that He was not going to fight, they ran away. Then the soldiers marched Jesus off to the city.

—*Matthew 26:30-50*

Jesus on Trial

Most of the people in Jerusalem were asleep. But in one house a group of men were waiting for Jesus. That was the high priest's house. Inside were seventy men trying to find witnesses who would lie about Jesus. Then it would be easy to go to the Roman governor and ask him to put Jesus to death. But even though some men agreed to tell lies, they did not make good witnesses. The witnesses could not agree in their lying! Finally, two men agreed to say, "This Man said that He was able to destroy God's Temple and build it again in three days."

The chief priest said to Jesus, "I demand that You tell me whether you have said that You are the Son of God."

"Yes," said Jesus, "I am. And I tell you that in the life to come you will see Me sitting at the right side of God."

When the chief priest heard this, he said, "What more do we need to prove that this Man is guilty and should die?" Some of the other men spit on Jesus. They hit Him as they said, "Tell us who hit You that time."

Now when Jesus had been led off by the soldiers, Peter had been terribly afraid. But when he saw that the soldiers were not interested in capturing the disciples, some of his courage came back. He decided to follow the mob to see what they would do to Jesus. When Peter came to the chief priest's house, he went into the courtyard where some servants were gathered around a fire.

As Peter was sitting near the fire to keep warm, a girl came over to him. "Say," she said, "you were with Jesus, weren't you?"

But Peter said, "I wasn't! I don't even know

what you are talking about!"

Then later on another servant girl noticed him and said, "This fellow was with Jesus."

"No!" screamed Peter. "I don't know Him."

After awhile some of the men servants came over to Peter. "Look," they said, "we know you are one of His disciples."

Again Peter said, "I don't even know the Man!" Just as Peter was talking, a rooster crowed. Then Peter sadly remembered what Jesus had said.

When morning came, the seventy rulers still didn't know what to do about Jesus. They decided to take Him to the Roman governor, Pilate.

As the rulers, some soldiers, and the Prisoner, Jesus, walked along, other people followed. When they reached the palace where the Roman governor lived, Pilate came out to the courtyard to talk to them.

"What has this Man done?" he asked.

"Well, sir," one of the rulers said, "if He had not done anything wrong, we would not be bothering you."

Pilate said, "Well, take Him. Judge Him by your law."

"We can't," said the ruler. "You know our law says that we cannot put any man to death. You have to do that."

Then Pilate went into his judgment hall. He asked the soldiers to bring Jesus to him.

"Are You the King of the Jews?" Pilate asked.

"Are you asking this for yourself," said Jesus, "or is this what others have told you?"

"Well, I'm not a Jew," said Pilate. "Your people have turned You over to me. What have You done?"

Jesus said, "I am not an earthly King. If I were, My friends would have fought the soldiers who captured Me. My kingdom is not in this world."

"Then You are a king?" questioned Pilate.

"You say that I am a King. Yes, for this reason I was born. I came into this world to tell people the truth."

"What is the truth?" Pilate asked. Then he went out to the rulers and said, "This Man is not guilty of any crime. But you have a custom. At Passover time you ask me to release someone from prison. I'll release Jesus."

"No! No!" screamed the people. "Not Jesus! Release the robber Barabbas!"

Then Pilate commanded that Jesus be beaten with a heavy whip. The soldiers put a crown of long

sharp thorns on His head. They put a purple robe on Him and made fun of Jesus by pretending to bow before Him. "Hail, 'King of the Jews!'" the soldiers screamed as they hit Him.

Pilate went back to the courtyard. "Now look," he said, "I have punished this Man, but I do not find Him guilty. I am going to bring Him out to you now."

Then Jesus came out wearing the crown of thorns and the purple robe. His back was bleeding, and His face had bruises where the soldiers had hit Him.

As soon as the people saw Jesus, they yelled, "Crucify Him! Crucify Him!"

Pilate said, "You kill Him. I do not find Him guilty!"

The Jewish rulers spoke up then, "By our law He ought to die, because He said that He is the Son of God!"

Then Pilate was afraid. He said, "Who are You? Do You know that I have the power to put You to death? Isn't there anything you can say so that I can set You free?"

Jesus said, "You would not have any power over Me if God didn't give it to you. Those men who have brought Me to you have sinned more than you have."

Finally, Pilate gave up. There seemed to be nothing more that he could do. He was afraid of the people and afraid of his own king, Caesar. "Take Him," Pilate said. And the Jews eagerly grabbed Jesus and led Him away.

—Matthew 26:57-75; John 18:28—19:16

Jesus Dies on the Cross

At last the Jewish rulers had Jesus in their power! Now they would put Him to death. Some of them brought a heavy wooden cross for Jesus to carry.

Many people stood along the sides of the streets as the soldiers dragged Jesus along. Some of them were crying. Jesus had healed many of them. He had talked with them about God. But now wicked men were taking Jesus to His death. No wonder the people cried! But no one dared to argue with the Jewish rulers and soldiers.

Finally, Jesus, the soldiers, and the crowd of people came to a hill outside the city of Jerusalem. This hill was known as "The Skull" or "Golgotha."

Here the soldiers nailed Jesus' hands and feet to the heavy cross He had been carrying. Two robbers were also nailed to crosses. Then the three crosses were lifted up and set in holes in the ground. This way of putting people to death was called "crucifixion."

"Father, forgive these people," Jesus said as He was hanging on the cross. "They don't know what they are doing."

The soldiers who crucified Jesus sat down to keep watch. They had to be sure that no one would try to take the three men down from the crosses.

Looking down from the cross, Jesus saw His mother standing with John. Jesus asked John to look after Mary. Then He asked Mary to think of John as her own son.

By this time it was noon, but suddenly the Earth was covered with darkness. It was as dark as the blackest night! And it stayed dark for three hours.

About three o'clock in the afternoon Jesus shouted, "My God, My God, why have You given Me up? Why have You left Me alone?"

At last Jesus said, "Father, into Your hands I give My Spirit." And then He died.

—*John 19:17-27; Matthew 27:33-50*

Jesus Is Buried

When evening came, Joseph of Arimathaea, one of Jesus' followers, went to Pilate. This rich man asked Pilate if he could take Jesus' body. He wanted to bury Jesus in his own rock tomb. Pilate gave the order, and Joseph took the body. He wrapped it in a clean linen cloth. Then he had his servants roll a huge stone in front of the door, or opening into the tomb.

Mary Magdalene and another woman named Mary were sitting near the tomb. They saw all that Joseph did. But the Jewish rulers began to worry when they heard that Jesus' body was in the tomb. They went to Pilate.

"Look," they said, "that Liar said that He was coming back to life after three days. We know He won't, but some of His friends may steal His body. Then they will say that Jesus came back to life. We need your help. We want an order from you to seal the tomb until the third day."

"Use your own Temple police," said Pilate. He did not seem to be too interested. "Your police can guard the tomb."

So the Jewish rulers sealed the tomb. Then they commanded some soldiers to watch.

—Matthew 27:57-66

Jesus' Last Days on Earth

Very early on the Sunday morning, when the Jewish Sabbath was over, and before it was really light, some women came to the tomb. The women —Mary Magdalene, Mary the mother of James, and Salome—were carrying perfumes to put around Jesus' body.

The sun was coming up by the time they reached Joseph of Arimathaea's garden and the tomb. "We shall not be able to roll the big stone away from the tomb," said one woman. They wondered who would help them.

But when they got to the tomb, they were sur-

prised because the stone had already been rolled away. Mary Magdalene was afraid. She ran away to tell some of the disciples. But the other women went to the doorway and looked in. The body of Jesus was not there! Suddenly they heard some wonderful news from an angel, who said, "Don't be afraid. I know that you are looking for Jesus. He is not here. He is alive again, as He said He would be."

Mary Magdalene did not hear this news because she hurried to Peter and John. When she found them, she said, "Oh, something terrible has happened! Someone has stolen our Lord's body!"

This news upset Peter and John. They wanted to see for themselves, so off they ran. John could run faster than Peter, but he waited at the tomb for Peter. Then the two men went inside. Mary Magdalene was right! The body was gone! They saw the linen cloth that had been wrapped around Jesus, but Jesus' body was nowhere to be seen. Sad and discouraged, the two men went home.

Mary Magdalene had followed the men to the tomb. But by the time she got there, Peter and John had left. Mary felt terrible. Jesus was dead! Mary was crying, but she decided to look inside the tomb. Inside the tomb she saw two angels sitting. "Why are you crying?" they asked her. "Because they have taken away my Lord. I don't know where they have put Him," Mary answered. And she went out from the tomb.

As she stood near the tomb, crying, she noticed Someone near her. That person said, "Why are you crying?" She thought it was the man who took care of the garden. "Oh," said Mary Magdalene, "if you have taken Him away, tell me where you put His body."

"Mary," said this One who was standing near her. Suddenly she knew His voice. Quickly Mary looked at Him. "Teacher!" she said. The Person was Jesus, who had come back to life.

"Mary," said Jesus, "go tell My friends that I am alive." So Mary hurried back to the city to tell the good news. "I have seen the Lord," she said. "He talked to me."

—Mark 16:1-6; John 20:1-18

Jesus Talks with Two Men

That same day, two of Jesus' followers were walking to the village of Emmaus, seven miles away from Jerusalem. As they walked along, they talked about Jesus' dying. Suddenly, Jesus Himself caught up with them and walked along with them. But they didn't know who He was.

"You seem to be talking about something very important," said Jesus. "What is it?"

The men stopped. One of them said, "Well, You must be the only One in all of Jerusalem that does not know what has happened. A terrible thing happened last week. Jesus, who did wonderful things by God's power, was crucified. The Jewish rulers made Pilate give the order to have Jesus killed. Now He is dead."

"Yes." said the other man, "all this is true. Then this morning some of the women who are also followers of Jesus went to the tomb. They came back with the news that Jesus' body was not in the tomb. They saw some angels there who said that Jesus is alive. Peter and John went to see for themselves. They, too, found the tomb empty."

"Don't you understand," said Jesus, "that the Scriptures tell you that the Saviour must die?" And Jesus repeated Scripture verses and explained what they said about Him.

By this time the two men were near Emmaus. They asked Jesus to stay all night with them. He agreed to eat supper with them, and after they sat down to eat, Jesus took the loaf of bread and asked God's blessing on it.

Suddenly, the two men knew who was eating with them. They saw that it was Jesus! But the very next minute He was gone. Jesus was alive! The men left their supper and hurried back to Jerusalem to tell the others that Jesus had talked with them.

When the men got back to the city and found the disciples, they told their story. And just as they were telling it, Jesus Himself was suddenly standing there with them. They were happy, but they were also afraid.

"Why are you afraid?" asked Jesus. "Don't you know Me? Look at My hands! Look at My feet." Then He held out His hands for them to see the marks that the nails had made. Then He said, "Do you have anything here to eat?" They gave Him a piece of baked fish, and He ate it.

Surely now the followers knew that the Man was God's Son, the Lord Jesus Christ.

Then Jesus began teaching them again. He explained many Scriptures. He said that the disciples should teach others. "Tell them," Jesus said, "that there is forgiveness of sins for all who turn to Me."

—Luke 24:13-47

Jesus Meets the Fishermen

Perhaps Jesus' disciples did not know how to begin teaching others. And because they did not know what to do, the men who had been fishermen went back to fishing. Seven of the men had gone back to the Sea of Galilee to catch fish and sell them.

"It's getting dark," said Peter as he stood on the lake shore with the other men. "I like to fish at night. I'm going fishing now."

"All right," said the six men, "we'll go with you." They all got into a large fishing boat, rowed out to deep water, and fished all night. But they did not catch one fish!

As the sky began to get light, they turned the boat toward shore and began to row. When they got close to land, they could see Someone standing on the shore. The disciples did not know who it was.

"What did you catch?" called the Man. "We didn't catch anything," one of the men shouted back.

Then Jesus said, "Look, stop where you are and put your net down on the right side of the boat." The men did as Jesus told them, and they could hardly pull the net up because it was so full of fish!

"It's the Lord!" said Peter as he jumped into the water. Peter could not wait for the boat to get to shore. He wanted to see Jesus right away.

When all of the men reached shore, they saw that Jesus had breakfast ready for them. There were some fish cooking over a fire of coals. And there was bread ready for them to eat.

Jesus said, "Come on and eat."

After breakfast, Jesus asked Peter three times if he loved Him. Three times Peter had said that he did not even know Jesus. Now Jesus gave him a chance to say three times that He did love Him. Peter said, "Lord, you know everything. You know that I love You!" Then Jesus said, "Look after My people who love Me."

—*John 21:1-17*

75

Jesus Goes Back to Heaven

The day had come for Jesus to return to heaven. Now His followers must carry on His work.

"You have seen how Scripture promises have come true," said Jesus. "You know how I died and came back to life again. Now you are to tell other people. Tell them that God will forgive the sin of all who ask Him and who believe in Me.

"I am going back to My Father, but I will send the Holy Spirit to you, just as My Father promised. Don't start your teaching yet. Stay here in Jerusalem until the Holy Spirit comes and gives you power from heaven."

Then Jesus led His disciples out from the city. He lifted up His hands and blessed them. And then Jesus began rising into the sky. He went on and on, out of their sight.

While the disciples were looking up into the sky watching Jesus, two angels stood with them. They said, "Why are you standing here looking at Jesus as though you are never going to see Him again? Someday He is going to come back from heaven in the very same way you see Him going to heaven."

The disciples were glad for this promise. They returned to Jerusalem to wait for the Holy Spirit, just as Jesus had told them to do.

It was a special day when the Holy Spirit came, the Day of Pentecost. All of the believers were in one house. They were praying and praising God when suddenly they heard a noise like a strong wind. Then what looked like flames of fire appeared and seemed to rest on the head of each one. And everyone was filled with the Holy Spirit and received power from Him. Because there were people in Jerusalem from many countries, the Holy Spirit gave the disciples power to speak many languages. Every person could hear the good news about Jesus in his own language.

When the people in Jerusalem heard what had happened, they were surprised. "How can these people speak other languages?" they asked. "These people live here and in Galilee, but they are talking in the languages of Egypt and Arabia and Persia and other places in Asia!"

Then Peter stepped forward and shouted, "Listen, I will tell you what has happened. God has given us His Holy Spirit, just as He promised in the Scriptures." Peter explained many Scriptures to the people. He preached a long sermon.

Peter closed his sermon by saying, "Each of you must turn from sin, ask God to forgive you. Trust in Jesus!" About three thousand people believed what Peter said and joined the group of Jesus' followers.

—*Luke 24:44-51; Acts 1:9-11; 2:1-11, 14, 38-41*